THE PERILS OF THE PUSHY PARENTS

THE PERILS
OF THE
PUSHY PARENTS

A CAUTIONARY TALE

Written and illustrated by
BORIS JOHNSON

Harper*Press*
An Imprint of HarperCollins*Publishers*

HarperCollins*Publishers*
77–85 Fulham Palace Road, Hammersmith, London W6 8JB

www.harpercollins.co.uk

Published by HarperCollins*Publishers* 2007
1

A catalogue record for this book is available from the British Library

ISBN 978-0-00-726339-4

Set in Bodoni

Printed and bound in Great Britain by Clays Ltd, St Ives plc

Mixed Sources

Product group from well-managed
forests and other controlled sources
www.fsc.org Cert no. SW-COC-1806
© 1996 Forest Stewardship Council

FSC is a non-profit international organisation established to promote the
responsible management of the world's forests. Products carrying the FSC
label are independently certified to assure consumers that they come
from forests that are managed to meet the social, economic and
ecological needs of present and future generations.

Find out more about HarperCollins and the environment at
www.harpercollins.co.uk/green

I

The nicest kids you ever saw
Were Jim and Molly Albacore,
Who seldom made a naughty noise
Or screamed for more expensive toys.

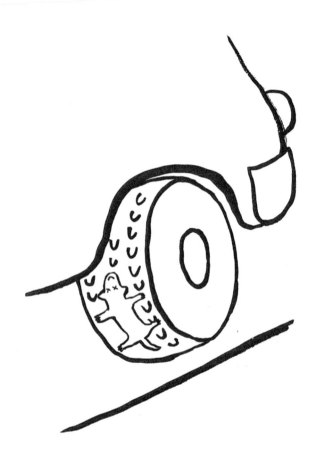

Indeed, they hardly ever cried,

Except when once a hamster died.

If they fought they made it up,
And if they broke a plate or cup,
They'd both confess at once and say,
'I think we've saved enough to pay!'

They brushed their teeth and scrubbed their toes.

They very rarely picked their nose,

And kept each other free of nits

By using little grooming kits.

In summer from the peep of dawn

They gambolled on the tiny lawn

In scenes of perfect bourgeois ease

With lavender and bumblebees

And games involving bits of string
Or planks of wood, or anything.
And yet, of course, when winter came,
The garden wasn't quite the same.

At dusk and having time to kill
What they liked to do was chill,
And get some lovely sliced white bread,
Then smear it thick with peanut spread,
Then cover that with strawberry jelly
And scoff it all before the TELLY.
Oh, how they loved that warm machine,

Its friendly, wise, hypnotic screen.
It never moaned at them or swore
Or yelled at them to shut the door.
Or taught them long division sums
Or told them not to scratch their bums
Or asked them in that maddening way,
'Darling, what did you DO today?'

Oh no, their television set
Would never carp at them or fret,
But delved into its mighty brain
To give, and give, and give again.
It gave them Friends and Dr Who
And dancing comps and Scooby Doo,

And wacky gameshows from Japan
In which contestants take a flan
Or piece of pie, and shout 'Banzai',
And chuck it in the other's eye,
So provoking gales of mirth
From all the children of the earth.

It gave them lumps of TV fun,

Baked and sweetened, every one,

Edible, digestible,

And slowly irresistible.

Sometimes when the coast was clear

They'd plug the console in the rear,

And play without a hint of shame

The latest electronic game.

Did anything detract from this
Condition of domestic bliss?
Was there a thorn, was there a weed in
Jim and Molly's childhood Eden?

There was. I crave your kind forbearance:
It's time to talk about the PARENTS.

II

The source, my friends, of half life's trouble

Is seeking reputation's bubble,

And though the kids were not ambitious –

Their beds were soft, their food delicious –

Their lives were not entirely cushy:

Their parents were so very pushy.

When they looked on Jim and Molly

(I say this with some melancholy)

They missed the pair of happy moochers

And saw a brace of 'brilliant futures'.

Let's take the father. What a freak!

His balding brow and lean physique

Concealed a terrifying zest

For putting children to the test.

When they were babies in the womb

He'd read them Berkeley, Locke and Hume.

Before their eyes were even open

He'd hum them bits of Bach and Chopin,

And not content, this massive swot,

Would teach them physics in the cot

And swipe away their infant bottle

And fill their hands with Aristotle.

When normal kids are doing well
To stick a bit of pasta shell
On card, or play with coloured blocks
He taught them Zeno's paradox!

Every year it grew intenser:
At five he put them down for Mensa.
At six he made them, lass and lad,
Contest a maths Olympiad
Which venture meeting mixed success
He'd wake them up with cries of 'Chess!'

When most of us are feeling weak.

Then after half an hour of Greek

He'd keep them in the chairs they sat in,

Switch their books and yell out, 'Latin!'

Something told him they would star

In ballet or in opera,

So with the zeal of ancient Sparta

He drilled them for La Traviata.

He'd make them play the violin

Then tell them with a sickly grin,

Containing just a hint of menace,

'February's great for tennis.

Come and meet your tennis teacher.

Come on, kids, say pleased to meet ya!'

Poor Jim and Molly did their best,

And yet they knew the vital test

For dad, more vital than a course
In how to serve or ride a horse,
Was quenching his hormonal need
To watch his little children READ.

The surest way of pleasing him

Was sitting like two cherubim

In silence and for simply ages

Rustling slowly through the pages.

Until he'd spot them, stop, and look,

32

And gasp, 'My word – they've got a book!'

He'd hide behind the door to spy.

A tear would glisten in each eye.

He'd hug himself. He'd cut a caper:

'They're reading printed words on paper!'

So how do you think his children could

Deprive him of his joyful mood?

You've got it. When he saw each loafer

Sitting drugged upon the sofa,

Their cheeks aglow with telly light,

His fuse would blow like gelignite.

His brow would bulge, his ears turn red.

'Why can't you read a book instead?'

And with a gargle in his throat

He'd make a grab for the remote.

He'd zap the programme off and holler

'Go and read some Emile Zola!'

III

Now if you think the dad was sad

Their darling MUM was twice as bad.

What was her method? Let me see.

She was a human JCB.

Her concept of maternal love

Was giving kids a whopping shove.

No elephant or heavy horse
Could match her for kinetic force
And as for scrumming toe to toe
She'd squish the All Black second row.

One Christmas in the usual way
The school put on a touching play
To mark Our Lord's nativity.
Young Molly was enthralled to be
Elected by her cheering class
To play the rear end of the ASS.

'What DO you mean?' cried Molly's mum.

'They've made you act a donkey's bum?

How dare they force my little lass

To imitate an ass's ass?

We rather hoped the BBC

Would hire you as a news trainee,

And after that it's our intent

To shove you into parliament,

Up the greasy pole – and then

Propel you into Number 10!

But as it is, your school, God rot 'em,

Portrays you as some dobbin's bottom.

What kind of university

Wants "donkey bum" on your CV?'
Before the girl could disabuse her
Mum had found the show's producer
And as a stork devours a frog
She seized the trembling pedagogue.
Quite what she whispered in his ear
I cannot say, and yet I fear
It must have been extremely scary.
He sacked the pupil playing Mary
And handing her a donkey's tail
He hushed her unbelieving wail:
'Can it, kiddo, you're a goner.
We're casting Molly as Madonna!'

Now if that story makes you sweat,
Amigos, you've seen nothing yet.

I'll make you wince. I'll make you squirm,
I'll tell you how one autumn term
Dear Jim just missed the football team.
His mum's reaction was EXTREME.

A shadow passed before her face –
Jim! Cheated of his rightful place.
A team without her gifted nipper!
She clutched her chest; she had a gripper.

At length she mastered her emotions

And like some DREADNOUGHT of the oceans,

Or like some mighty Task Force, she
Steamed towards her enemy.
She reached the school and Oh! the shame,
She stormed the pitch and stopped the game!

And spoke in terms of harsh reproach
To both the teacher and the coach.
Soon Jim was back and some poor titch
Ejected weeping from the pitch,

And then she glared a fearful glare

At all the parents standing there.

And my! how little Jimmy blushed

To see the way his mother PUSHED.

Alas the worst was yet to come

From pushy dad and pushy mum.

Though each alone was pretty tough,

When they got together – OOF!

IV

That very night at half-past nine
They opened up some nice red wine,
And thinking both the kids in bed
The barmy pair went head to head
Upon the kitchen tabletop.
Like Molotov and Ribbentrop

Deciding on the fate of nations,

They made initial preparations

For what they thought a harmless plot

That very nearly KILLED THE LOT!

Down the stairs the children stole

And cupped their ears about the hole.

They held their breath to overhear;

Their brows turned white in very fear.

'I tell you what,' they heard mum say,

'Let's have a really special day.

Let's make all the neighbours see

Our massive generosity.'

Through the door's vibrating wood

The children swiftly understood.

Consumerism's worst result

Has been the terrifying cult

That turns our parents by degrees

Into drug-crazed votaries

Who slash their veins without a wail

Before this all-consuming Baal,

This god more greedy than Astarte,

The fetish of the children's party!

'Agreed,' said dad, 'let's turn them green.

Let's make them feel all pinched and mean.

What kind of party shall we throw?

Sleepovers went out years ago,

And chaps with snakes, I'm sad to say,

Like conjurers, are quite passé.

The People's Circus of Beijing

Is suddenly not quite the thing.

Paintballing? A football match?

No, none of these are up to scratch.'

'We need,' mused mum, 'a novel theme

For little Molly's birthday dream.'

She crooked an eyebrow as she spoke.

Was that a muffled childish croak

Behind the door? She frowned. But now

Dad yelped and smote his bulging brow.

'That's it! That's how our son and daughter

Can blow our rivals out the water.

It's big. It's brainy. It's bodacious!

It's arty and yet ostentatious:

A show to make our neighbours ill,

A birthday party by De Mille!

Let's put a ballet on and make

Them all watch Molly in Swan Lake!'

'You've got it!' mum exclaimed. 'Hurrah!

And Jim can lead the orchestra.

We've got two months; it's not too late.

We'll coach him up to pass Grade Eight.'

At this she leapt up from the table

And as fast as she was able

Flung wide the door and scanned the stair

And GRUNTED to see no one there.

V

The neighbourhood had never seen a
Proper prima ballerina
Like Olga Kleb from Belarus.
She turned up at the children's house
Prepared to make them physically
Ready to perform a ballet.

In a quite transparent grump

At teaching kiddies how to jump

She launched herself upon a mean

Red Army-style warm-up routine.

She stretched her hams, and flexed her joints

And twirled upon her tiptoe points.

After eighty bunny hops

She showed them her karate chops,

'And now!' she barked, 'I show the use

Of a pair of ballet shoes.

They must be clean like mine, and neat

And fit most tight around the feet.'

She tried hers on. Her marrow froze.

Something SQUELCHED between her toes.

She gave a squeak and tried to jump

And yank her foot from out the pump.

Alas, too late: the dainty shoe

Was stuck on fast with loving goo.

So bending neatly at the waist
She gave the yellow gunk a taste;
And whispered with a broken stutter,
'It's P-p-P-p-Peanut butter!'
She fled the house and nevermore
Came back to dance chez Albacore.

And if you grieve for her then wait

And hear the quite appalling fate

Delivered by some secret djinn

To him who taught the violin.

Now after he had scraped the fiddle

This honest dope desired a widdle;

And when he'd done this trifling job

He tried the door – and found no knob!

He gave a push; he gave a wail:

The toilet had become his jail.

He snarled, he bit, he scratched, he kicked it.

I think he may have even licked it;

And pretty soon the crazy loon
Was doggy-howling at the moon.

Two hours or more it must have been
Before the parents found the scene.
As soon as they had turned the locks
They heard the chatter of the box;

But, louder far, the upstairs bog

Appeared to hide a rabid dog.

Quick! Quick! They sprang the poor musician

And gasped to see his changed condition.

His alabaster hands were sore

From scratching at the toilet door.

Streaks of tears ran down his face;

His silk cravat was out of place.

He hadn't quite yet lost his mind.

Before he fainted he resigned,

And gave a kind of punctured sigh.

They looked each other in the eye

Then from downstairs they heard the roar:

The telly! louder than before!

They worked it out at once, and WHAM,

Rage hit them in the diaphragm.

Two minds with but a single goal.

Four eyeballs glowing like hot coal.

Eight limbs united on one mission:

To MARMALISE the television!

They had no time to form a plan;

Rage armed them quickly as they ran.

While mum picked up a frying pan,

That was no weapon for a man,

Thought dad. No, no, this drama

Would climax with a great big HAMMER.

VI

With a slow and wondering glance
The children look up from their trance.
They see the threat. They scream. They scram.
They leave their peanut spread and jam
And hunt for refuge while they can
From sledgehammer and frying-pan,
As with a petrifying roar
Dad holds his hammer high like Thor!

Like Hector in the Achaean ships

A battle-cry escapes his lips.

His eyeballs bulge, his forehead, too.

A jagged vein is pulsing blue.

He whirls his hammer round and round.

He makes a funny clicking sound.

And with a shocking sickening crash

He deals a heavy forehand smash,

Then grips the hammer like an axe

And gives that telly forty whacks,

And when she sees what he has done

Mum gives the console forty-one!

And to and fro, and to and fro

They biff like Borg and McEnroe

Until those merry kids' machines

Are smashed to tiny smithereens

And dad is standing in a puddle

Of TV guts and other muddle;

And crunching on the broken glass

He moves in for the coup de grace.

And as he takes that final swing

A small voice sighs, 'Goodbye, old thing',

As if a friend were dying, or

As if a much-loved Labrador,

Were flattened by a passing lorry.

Dad blinks. He gulps. He's almost sorry.

The contradiction makes him flip.

He's lost control; he's had a blip!

The children watch the hammer slip

From their father's nerveless grip

And like a streaking missile zoom

Silently across the room

Where mum is beating merry hell
Out of the mobile phones as well
And doesn't even spot the hazard
But cops it squarely on the mazard.

VII

Six weeks have passed. The family
Has come to Bournemouth, where the sea
Is lilac blue; upon the breeze
The whiff of scones and strawberries.
All about the sparkling bay
OTHER FAMILIES laugh and play,
And on the biscuit-coloured sand
Happy dots walk hand in hand.

But now let's make a sudden swoop
To focus on our tragic group,
Whose mood is frankly far from jolly.
We zoom in first on Jim and Molly.

With aching legs and straining backs
And grunting like a brace of yaks
And puffing hard at every yard
Up the clifftop promenade
With tender and exquisite pains
They tote their parents' sad remains.

Behold them, reader, and despair:

Their lolling eyes, their glassy stare,

This formerly dynamic pair

In a double-seat wheelchair.

Behold the mum, and see! A fly
Has landed boldly by her eye
And quite unchastened now it goes
To see what's up inside her nose.
Her brain, alas, can barely boast
The cunning of a piece of toast.
And as for dad's IQ, poor soul,
It's lower than a sausage roll.

The voices of command are hushed.

The pushy have become the pushed.

At last they reach the topmost crest,

Where Jim and Molly take a rest

And flop upon the springy grass

To watch the fleecy cloudlets pass

While mum and dad (it's just too cruel)

Gaze silently to sea and DROOL.

Jim starts to sleep, and in his dream

Conceives a labour-saving scheme.

In common with that sis of his

He's learnt the myth of Sisyphus,

And though it almost made them pop

To push their parents to the top

He knows that of its own free will

The wheelchair will proceed downhill...

Before he gets his brain in gear

Or common sense can interfere

He stretches out a gentle toe

To try to make that wheelchair go!

In later years old men will say

That they were on the cliffs this day

And when the kids sit goggle-eyed

About the fire at Christmas-tide

They'll badger Grandpa to enlarge
Upon the wheelchair's final charge.
'Go on!' they'll plead, with beating hearts,
'Tell us how the death-ride starts!'

'Aha,' he'll answer, 'truth to tell,

Jim's scheme begins by going well.'

While mum and dad stare into space
The wheelchair glides at walking-pace,
With Jim and Molly quite content
To trust it to the gradient.
But then – I don't know what – some rock
Gives the chair a bump or shock,

And with that jolt the parents bolt –

And gallop like a bee-stung colt.

Children scream and drop their ices

Off the hungry precipices.

Women faint and clifftop voles
Shoot in terror down their holes
And kissing couples stop to blench
And topple backwards off their bench
And crowds of halfwits stand and cheer
The Pushy Parents' mad career;

And still they thunder on downhill
To where a figure stands stock-still,
Waiting where the path grows steeper:
A hooded figure! Aaargh! The Reaper!

But no – it's just some harmless twit

Cowled up in his running kit,

So deaf he hears them far too late.

He gasps. He has a choice of fate:

He's either splattered on the course

Or else he jumps into the gorse.

He jumps, poor fool, and on they rush,

Past the faintly moaning bush,

Towards a nasty hairpin bend.

And surely this must be the end?

Or can the lean and faithful steed

Corner at such dreadful speed

And can the elder Albacores

Succeed in breaking Nature's laws

By sticking in the wheelchair while it

Turns on automatic pilot?

Might they? Can they? Will they? Nope.

The clifftop watchers lose all hope.

Like some bounding antelope

The wheelchair-jockeys clear the slope,

And in that instant something stirs

Inside their heads. A sprocket whirs.

Their brains switch on, their eyes demist,

They realise that they still exist.

The pushy pair regain their sight!

They give a primal scream of fright

To see the wheelchair launch itself

Off the clifftop's grassy shelf,

Where jagged boulders wait beneath

With lots of jagged little teeth…

Just when they brace themselves for death

A hand shoots out from on the heath

And with a grip of whippy steel

It grabs the wheelchair by the wheel

And breaks its fall, and lets it swing:

A conker on a human string

Consisting of their first-born, Jim,

And Molly holding on to him

And holding Molly from the edge

A Bournemouth taxi-man called Reg.

VIII

We meet a little later on.

The victory picnic's nearly done

And each parent and each child

All alike are reconciled.

The father looks around his team

And once again his eyeballs GLEAM.

He bounces to his feet to boast

In tones that echo up the coast:

'My friends, it's clear that our salvation

Has been our children's education!

Thank God their little heads are packed

With yards and yards of vital fact.

That's what taught them what to do –

All that maths, and physics, too,

And geometry, and all you need

To calculate a wheelchair's speed.

Yes, unless I'm much mistaken,

My coaching has brought home the bacon!'

He stops, and much to his surprise

'What rubbish!' little Molly cries.

'Dad, you haven't understood
The golden rules of Hollywood.

In any scene of hot pursuit

The hero first gives chase on foot

Till fate supplies a miracle –

Someone else's vehicle,

And then we watch the hero grab

Some bike or plane or taxicab

And in that cab, the script insists,

He apprehends the terrorists.

And, darling dad, I have to say

That's roughly what took place today.

It's not the fruit of your tuition.

We got it from the TELEVISION.'

A deadly pause. The children wait

For mum and dad to detonate.

They note the symptoms that presage

A bout of high parental rage:

A sudden gulping in the gullet

Like a quite offended mullet;

The way the mouth snaps wide and shut

As modelled on a halibut;

The creases in the brows that show

A pair of whales about to blow.

They're going any second now...

They're gonna pop, I tell you – POW!

And then indeed the Albacores
Explode – but into wild applause!
They howl and pant and hoot and shriek.
They laugh and laugh until they're weak.
And when the pair can laugh no more
Up stands Mrs Albacore

Upon the desert of the beach

To make a last impassioned speech:–

'Pushy parents everywhere!

Contemplate this mangled chair!

Cringe at how its wheel was bent

In that so-called accident.

One misguided little push

Nearly turned us both to mush.

Let's be honest, let's not fudge –

Let's explain that subtle nudge.

Let's go back to Sigmund Freud:

Was a part of Jim annoyed?

Did some deep subconscious bate

Drive him to reciprocate?

Did his darling ma and pa

Try to push him just too far?

Maybe sometimes it's a sin

Trying to force our kids to win.

Maybe pushing them ahead

Helps to cheese them off instead.

Even if your life's a bitch

Watching all your friends get rich,

Isn't it a kind of cheat

Using children to compete?

Let them breathe and let them be;

Let's not live vicariously.

All the pushing that you do –

Who's it helping, them or you?

Every child's a human being,

Not a piece of Plasticine.

Loving parents, learn from me.

If your children crave TV

Tell them, OK, what the hell,

You can watch it for a spell…

IF YOU READ A BOOK AS WELL.

(A proper book, you'll understand,

Like the volume in your hand.)